INSIDE AN EGG

by Sylvia A. Johnson

Photographs by Kiyoshi Shimizu

A Lerner Natural Science Book

Lerner Publications Company ▪ Minneap...

Sylvia A. Johnson, Series Editor

Translation of original text by Chaim Uri

Drawings on pages 17, 22, 26, and 33 by James R. Smail

The publisher wishes to thank James R. Smail,
Professor of Biology, Macalester College,
for his assistance in the preparation of this book.

LIBRARY OF CONGRESS CATALOGING IN PUBLICATION DATA

Johnson, Sylvia A.
  Inside an egg.

  (A Lerner natural science book)
  Adaptation of: Tamago no himitsu: by Kiyoshi
Shimizu.
  Includes index.
  Summary: Text and photographs trace the develop-
ment of a chicken egg from the time it is laid until the
chick is born.
  1. Chick embryo—Juvenile literature. [1. Chick em-
bryo. 2. Eggs] I. Shimizu, Kiyoshi, 1924- ill. II.
Shimizu, Kiyoshi, 1924- Tamago no himitsu. III. Title.
IV. Series.
QL959.J74   598'.617   81-17235
ISBN 0-8225-1472-9 (lib. bdg.)   AACR2

This edition first published 1982 by Lerner Publications Company.
Text copyright © 1982 by Lerner Publications Company.
Photographs copyright © 1975 by Kiyoshi Shimizu.
Adapted from THE SECRETS OF THE EGG copyright © 1975 by Kiyoshi Shimizu.
English language rights arranged by Kurita-Bando Literary Agency
for Akane Shobo Publishers, Tokyo, Japan.

International Standard Book Number: 0-8225-1472-9
Library of Congress Catalog Card Number: 81-17235

1 2 3 4 5 6 7 8 9 10 90 89 88 87 86 85 84 83 82

Have you ever seen baby chickens hatching from their eggs? It is exciting to watch while a chick pushes and pecks its way out of the egg shell, chirping loudly all the time. It is just as exciting to watch the development of a chick during the 21 days that it spends in the egg before it hatches. By means of the photographs in this book, you will be able to see the different stages in this remarkable development, which transforms a tiny cluster of cells into a fluffy, bright-eyed chick.

The first stage of this development takes place inside the body of a female chicken, or **hen.** This is where eggs are produced.

The part of the egg that we usually call the yolk is formed in the hen's **ovary.** The ovary contains many yolks in different stages of growth. When one yolk becomes large enough, it bursts out of the ovary and moves into a tube called the **oviduct.** As the yolk travels along the oviduct, the two other basic parts of the egg form around it—first the clear substance that surrounds the yolk, known as **albumen** or egg white, and then the hard shell. About 24 hours after the yolk entered the oviduct, the completed egg is ready to be laid. It comes out of the hen's body through an opening called the **cloaca.**

This is the process of development that produces the eggs people use as food. But an egg that will hatch into a chick must go through one more important step. This requires the help of a male chicken, or **rooster.**

Like many other kinds of animals, chickens create more of their own kind through the process of sexual reproduction. This means that a new life is formed by the joining of two sex cells, one from the male animal and one from the female. In most animals, these special reproductive cells are very small, but the sex cell of a female chicken is quite large. In fact, what we call the yolk of an egg is actually a single female sex cell, or **ovum.**

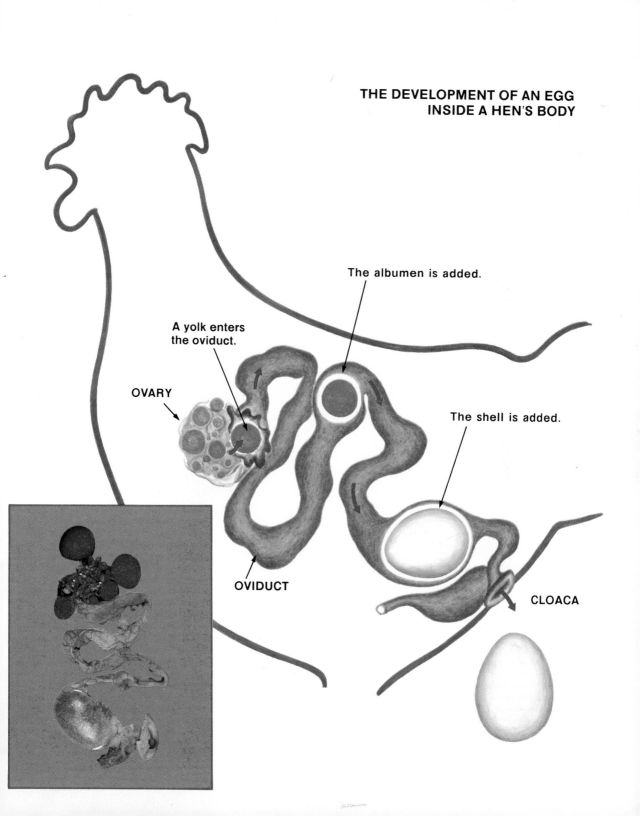

THE DEVELOPMENT OF AN EGG
INSIDE A HEN'S BODY

The albumen is added.

A yolk enters
the oviduct.

OVARY

The shell is added.

OVIDUCT

CLOACA

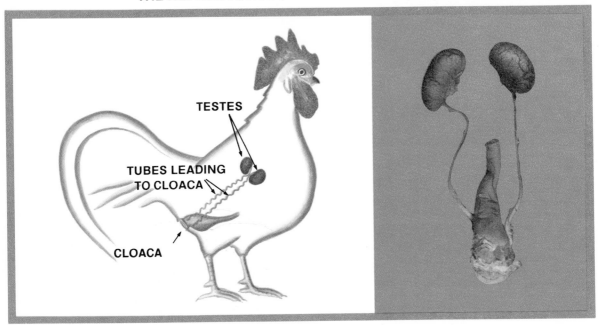

The ovum has two basic parts. The largest part is the orange yolk material, which contains food that can nourish a growing chick. The part of the ovum that will become the chick itself is the **nucleus,** a tiny speck on the surface of the yolk no bigger than a pinpoint.

In order for the ovum to develop into a chick, it must be united with a **sperm,** the male sex cell. Large numbers of sperm are produced by the **testes,** two small organs in the rooster's body. The tiny cells move through two tubes to an opening called the cloaca, just like the opening in the female's body.

When a hen and rooster mate, these two openings are brought together. Sperm pass from the male's body to the female's body, entering through the cloaca and moving into the oviduct. The sperm travel rapidly along the oviduct by wiggling their long, thin tails. In the upper part of the oviduct, a single sperm unites with the nucleus of an ovum that has burst out of the ovary. This union is called **fertilization,** and it is the beginning of a new life.

A hen and rooster mating. The rooster holds onto the hen's comb with his beak to keep his balance.

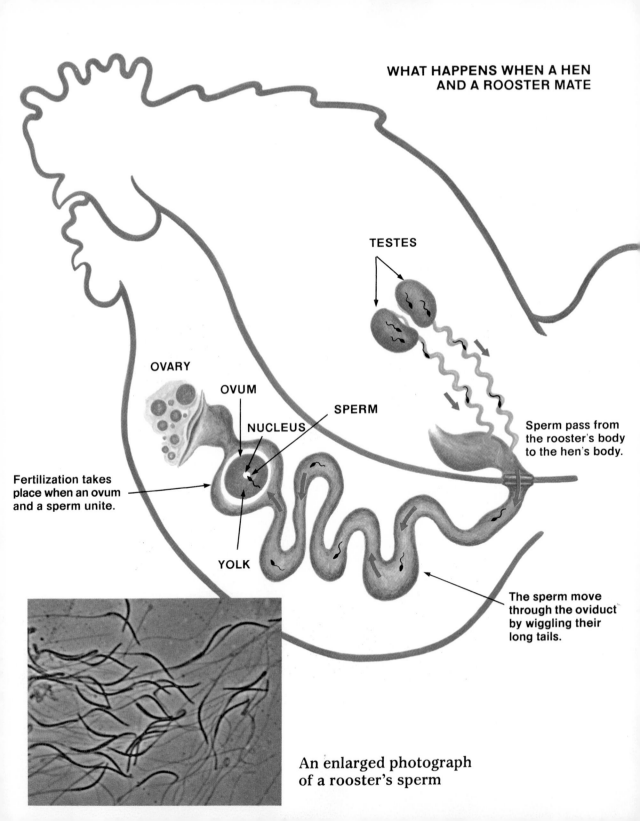

WHAT HAPPENS WHEN A HEN AND A ROOSTER MATE

TESTES

OVARY

OVUM

NUCLEUS

SPERM

Fertilization takes place when an ovum and a sperm unite.

YOLK

Sperm pass from the rooster's body to the hen's body.

The sperm move through the oviduct by wiggling their long tails.

An enlarged photograph of a rooster's sperm

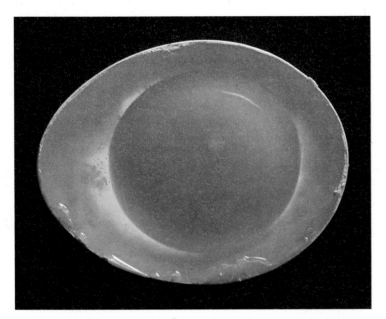
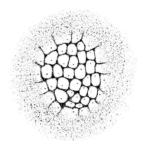
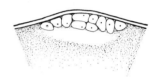

The faint white spot on the yolk of this egg is the cluster of cells that will develop into a chick. The drawing on the upper right shows the cluster as seen from above, enlarged about 10 times. The lower drawing is a cross-section of the top of the yolk showing the several layers that make up the cluster of cells.

As soon as fertilization takes place, cell division begins in the ovum. As the fertilized ovum moves through the oviduct, more and more new cells appear. The cells form a tiny cluster on the surface of the yolk material, which does not go through cell division. By the time the egg is laid, there are several layers of cells clustered together on the surface of the yolk. This tiny collection of cells is the first stage in the development of a chick.

Left:An electric incubator. *Right*: A snowy heron incubating her eggs with the heat from her body

In order to continue its development, the chick needs one very important thing: warmth. If an egg is not kept warm after it is laid, the cells on the yolk will stop growing. Female chickens, like most other birds, sit on their eggs to keep them warm. This is called **incubation.** People who raise thousands of chickens on farms use large machines called **incubators** to provide the warmth that eggs need to develop.

It takes 21 days of incubation for a chicken egg to hatch. If you take eggs from an incubator at different times during these 21 days and look inside them, you will be able to see the various stages of development that a chick goes through. By peeling away part of the egg shell very carefully, you can actually see the tiny speck of life growing on the surface of the yolk. An even better way to find out exactly what is happening is to take the developing chick from the egg, put it on a glass slide, and look at it through a microscope. The pictures in this book show chick development in both these ways.

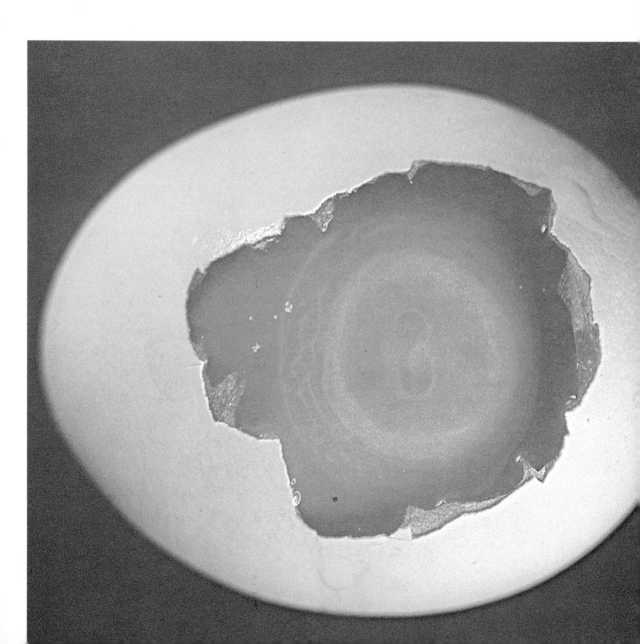

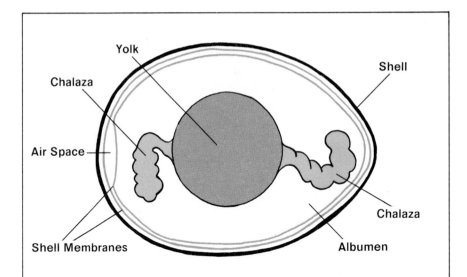

Yolk

Shell

Chalaza

Air Space

Chalaza

Shell Membranes

Albumen

INSIDE AN EGG All the parts of a chicken egg have a role to play in the chick's development. The *shell* is made of a strong material that protects the chick yet lets air in from the outside. Inside the shell are two thin skins or *membranes* that are separated from each other at the large end of the egg. The *air space* that forms between the two membranes plays an important role during the final days of the chick's development. The *albumen* or white of the egg creates a protective layer of fluid around the chick. It also serves as a source of food, just as the *yolk* does. Part of the albumen forms a rope-like structure called a *chalaza,* which is connected to each end of the yolk and acts as a kind of anchor. When the egg is turned over, the chalazas allow the yolk to turn too so that the developing chick can always remain on the top.

During the first hours of incubation, the cells that make up the chick go through many changes. The layers of cells that formed even before the egg was laid are starting to develop into the different parts of the chick's body. Now the collection of cells is called an **embryo,** a word used to describe all animals in this early stage of development.

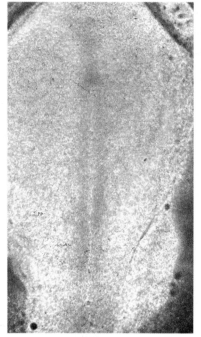 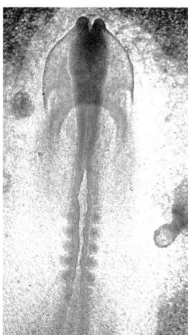

A 16-hour embryo   A 24-hour embryo

The picture on the left, taken through a microscope, shows an embryo that has been incubated for 16 hours. At this stage, all that can be seen of the embryo's body is a faint line about 2 millimeters (.08 inches) long. This line, called the **notochord,** marks the general area where the embryo's spinal cord will eventually form.

The picture on the right shows an embryo at 24 hours. The parts of the head have started to take shape, and on either side of the notochord, block-like clusters of cells called **somites** have begun to appear. As the embryo continues to develop, the cells of the somites will become the muscles and bones of its body.

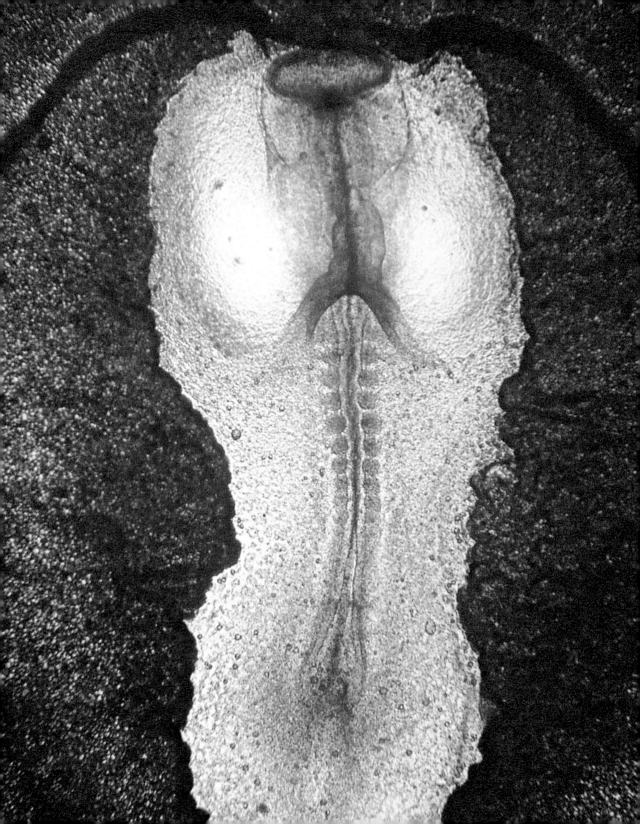

On the opposite page is a picture of an embryo that has been incubated for about 30 hours. It is 4 millimeters (.2 inches) long and has 10 pairs of somites. The embryo's head has begun to bulge out on both sides. These two bulges are the beginnings of its eyes. Another bulge farther down on the right side is the embryo's heart. Connected to it are large blood vessels that are the first stages of the circulatory system. Other blood vessels are developing in the area around the embryo, but at this stage, they are not yet connected to the embryo's body.

After about 38 hours of incubation, the embryo begins to change its position on the yolk. Starting at the head, its body gradually bends in a curve. At the same time, the embryo begins to turn so that its left side faces the yolk. The turning also starts in the area of the head and eventually includes the whole body.

These illustrations show an embryo that has been incubated for 48 hours. In the pictures on the opposite page, you can see how the embryo's body has begun to bend into a curve. The head is turned to the side, and below it is the heart, which is now shaped like a tube. Surrounding the embryo is a network of tiny blood vessels. In the picture below, the area covered by the blood vessels can be seen within the light red circle.

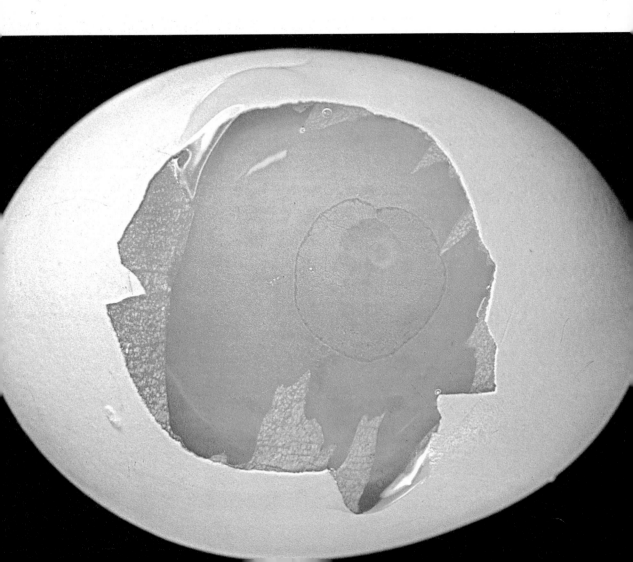

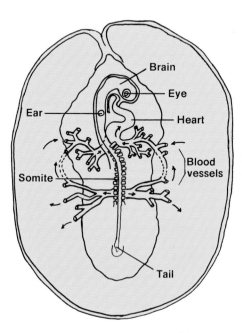

Brain

Eye

Ear

Heart

Somite

Blood vessels

Tail

After 48 hours of incubation, the upper part of the embryo's body has turned on its side. The eyes, ears, and brain have taken shape, and the circulatory system is developing.

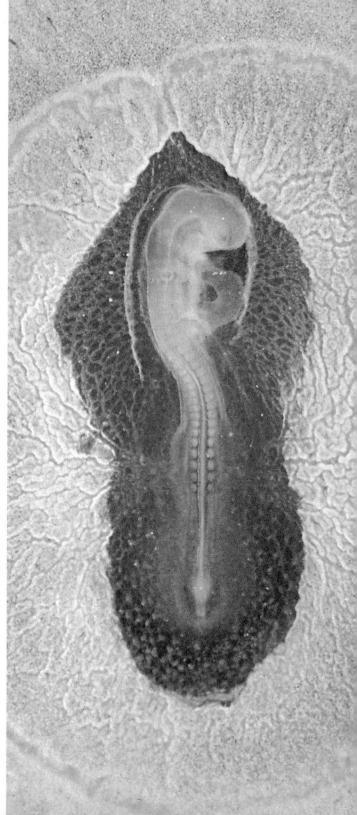

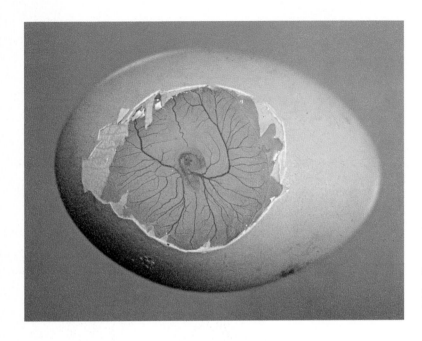

Left and opposite: An embryo incubated for 60 hours

By the time an embryo has been incubated for 60 hours, the blood vessels are much larger. If you open an egg at this stage of development, you can see them spread out in a bright red network across the yolk.

The small blood vessels that have been growing in the area around the embryo are now connected to the blood vessels in the embryo's body and to its heart. The heart itself is beating strongly, and you can easily see its movement in the opened egg. These strong heartbeats are circulating blood through the system of vessels, bringing food from the yolk into the embryo's body. Nourished by the proteins and other food materials in the yolk, the embryo will grow rapidly.

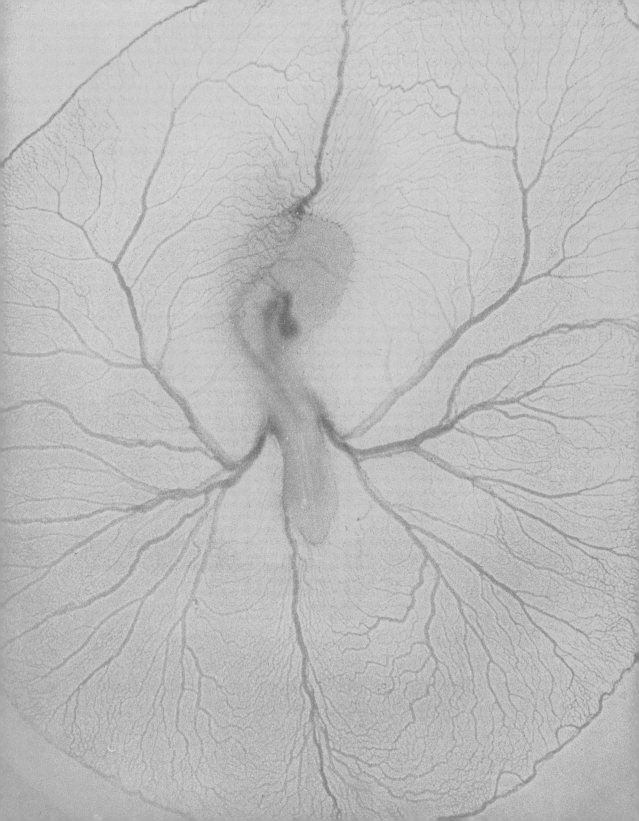

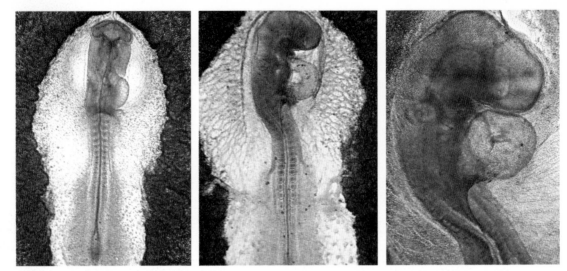

This series of pictures shows the development of the embryo's heart.

The embryo's heart has gone through many stages of development to reach the point where it is able to pump blood through the complicated circulatory system. In the pictures on these two pages, you can see some of the stages.

The picture above on the left shows an embryo at 35 hours. Its heart can be seen as a kind of bulge or swelling on the right side of its body. It has already begun beating, but the beats are slow and uneven. By the 48th hour of incubation, the heart is tube-shaped and its beats have become more regular (middle picture).

Between the 50th and the 70th hours of incubation, the tube-shaped heart twists and bends until it forms a kind of loop (right). The loop continues to twist and bend back on itself. At the same time, its walls squeeze together to form a partition.

By the time the embryo has been incubated for 100 hours (below), two separate chambers have taken shape in the heart. Later these two chambers—the atrium and the ventricle—will each be divided again to make four chambers.

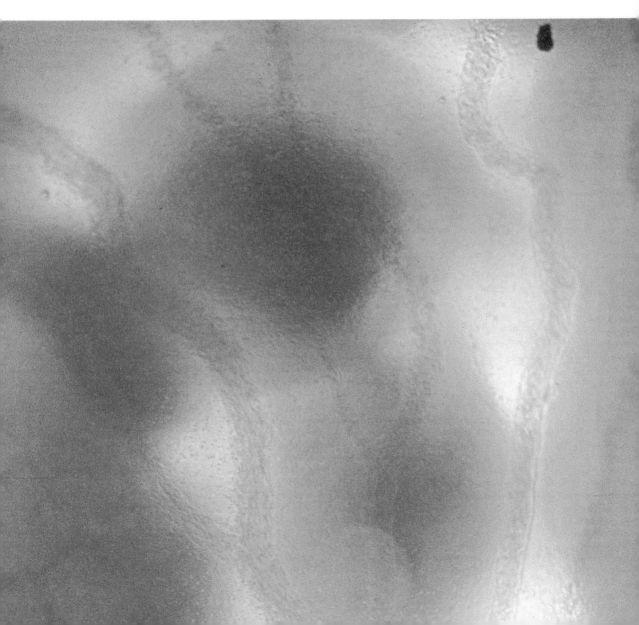

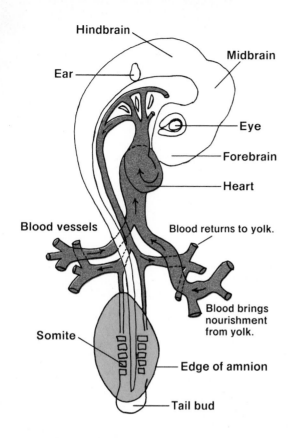

Hindbrain

Midbrain

Ear

Eye

Forebrain

Heart

Blood vessels

Blood returns to yolk.

Blood brings nourishment from yolk.

Somite

Edge of amnion

Tail bud

Opposite: A three-day embryo

Left: This diagram of a three-day embryo shows the three main parts of the brain and the blood vessels going to and from the yolk. The circular opening at the bottom, which can also be seen in the photograph, is the edge of the membrane called the *amnion.*

At the same time that the embryo's heart and circulatory system are developing, other parts of its body are changing and growing too. The brain is one of these parts.

The formation of an embryo's brain begins after about 27 or 28 hours of incubation. In the early stages of development, the brain is divided into three sections—the forebrain, the midbrain, and the hindbrain. As the embryo grows, these three sections will go through other divisions. By the time the embryo has been incubated for 72 hours, or three days, its brain has begun to form the five regions that are found in the brains of adult chickens and of all other animals with backbones.

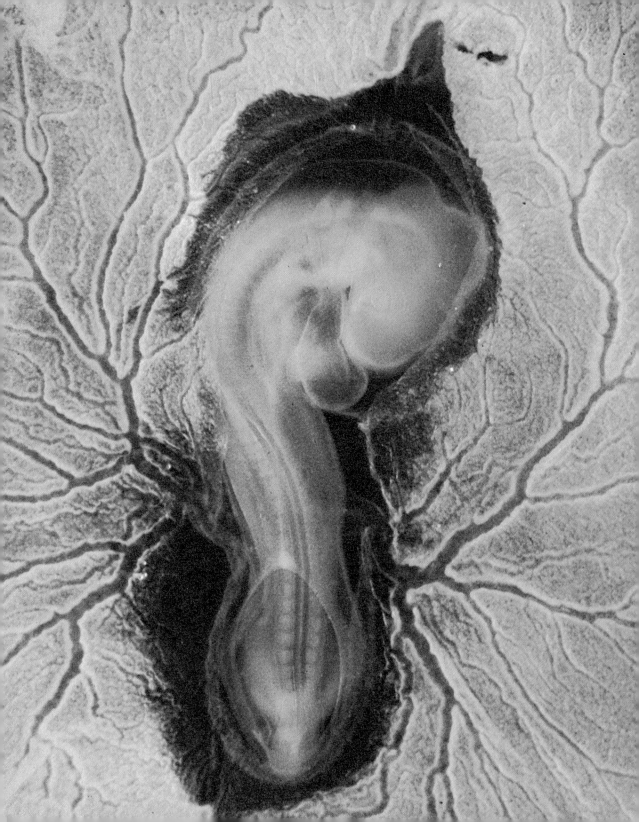

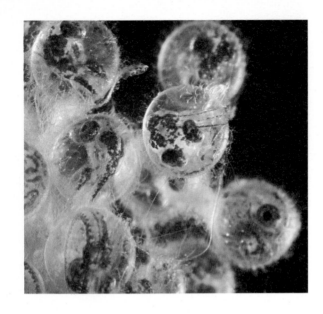

Protected by a transparent, jelly-like covering, these killifish embryos go through many of the same stages of development as a chick embryo in its hard-shelled egg.

An embryo that has been incubated for three days has gone through many changes, but it still doesn't look very much like a chicken. In fact, a chick embryo at this stage of development looks more like the embryos of other animals than like an adult chicken.

The pictures on these two pages show fish embryos in their jelly-like wrappings and a baby fish just after hatching. The developing fish with their large eyes and long tails have a lot in common with the chick embryos we have seen earlier. This is because chickens, fish, and all other animals with backbones—including humans—are very similar in the early stages of their development. Some embryos look so much like the embryos of other species that it is hard to tell them apart. But as the embryos grow, they begin to look more like their parents and less like their animal relatives.

After developing for 15 days, this killifish hatched from its protective covering. Attached to its body is a part of the egg yolk, which will continue to provide nourishment until the young fish can find its own food.

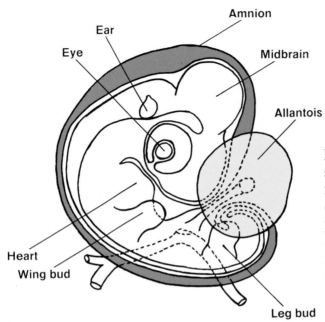

Amnion

Ear

Eye

Midbrain

Allantois

Heart

Wing bud

Leg bud

In this diagram, you can see some of the important features of the four-day embryo shown on the opposite page. The amnion and the allantois are two membranes that surround the embryo or are connected to it.

A great many changes take place between the third and fourth days of a chick embryo's incubation. By the end of the fourth day, the embryo's body has curled up so much that the head and tail areas are coming close together. The embryo's eyes have become very dark and can easily be seen. Wings and legs have also begun to grow, but at this time, they appear only as small bumps or buds on the embryo's body.

A very noticeable feature of a four-day embryo are the membranes that surround it or are connected to it. The sacks or capsules formed by the membranes serve an important purpose; they provide oxygen for the embryo and protect it from injury. Later in the book, you will learn more about the development and function of the membranes.

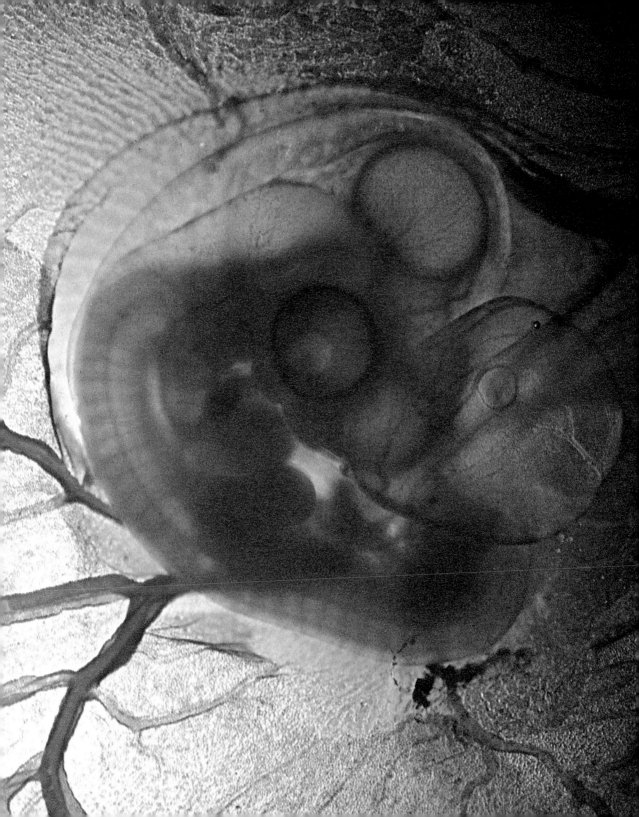

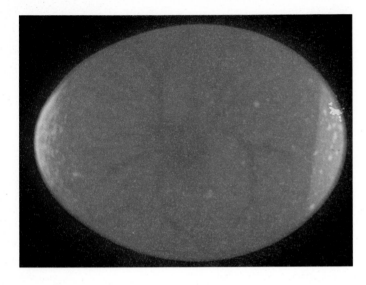

Opposite: A five-day embryo

Left: If you hold a six-day egg up to an electric light, you can see the many red blood vessels through the shell.

By the fifth day of incubation, the embryo is about 10 millimeters (.4 inches) long, and it has begun to move inside the shell. At this stage of development, the embryo needs an increasing amount of nourishment. The system of blood vessels that bring food from the yolk has grown in order to provide this nourishment. Many tiny blood vessels now surround the embryo and are connected to its body. This system of vessels almost covers the whole yolk.

The embryo is joined to the yolk not only by the complicated system of blood vessels but also by the **yolk stalk**. This is a thin section of the **yolk sac** (the membrane covering the yolk), which extends into the mid-section of the embryo's body. As the embryo grows, it uses more and more of the yolk. A few days before it is ready to hatch, only a small amount of yolk will remain, attached to the embryo's body by the yolk stalk.

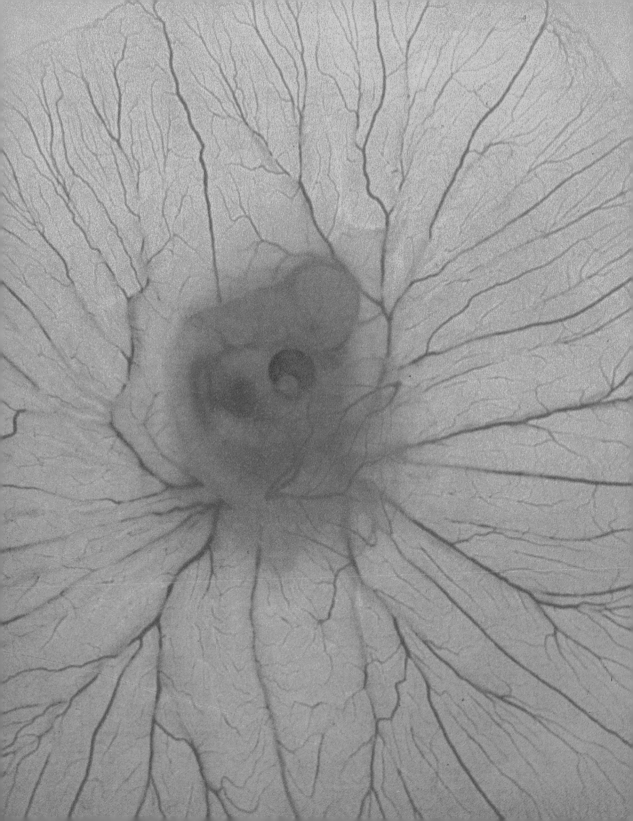

The eight-day embryo shown in the picture on the opposite page has been removed from the shell so that you can get a better look at a very important feature. This is the **amnion**, the transparent sack or capsule that surrounds the growing chick.

The amnion is a **membrane**, a very thin layer of cells. It first begins to develop when the embryo is only about 20 or 30 hours old. The amnion grows down from the top and gradually encloses the embryo's body. In the picture of a three-day embryo on page 23, the amnion has covered all but the very bottom part of the body. By the time that the embryo is four days old, it is completely surrounded by the amnion.

Inside the amnion is a watery liquid called the **amniotic fluid**. The embryo floats in this liquid, protected against injuries and against sudden changes in temperature.

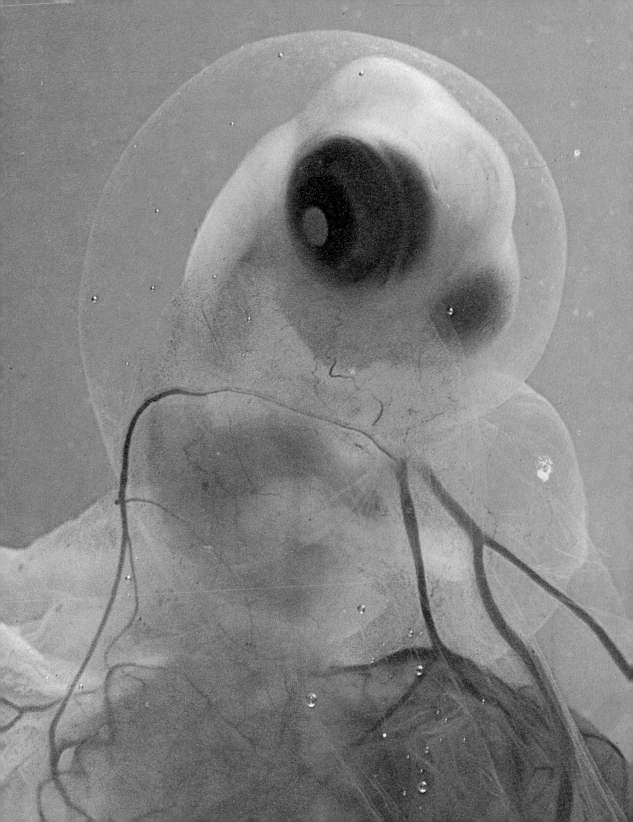

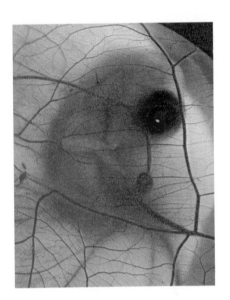

An 11-day embryo seen through
the transparent membrane of
the allantois

The amnion protects the embryo from being damaged by forces from outside the egg. Another membrane, the **allantois,** brings oxygen from outside the egg into the embryo's body.

The allantois begins its development inside the body of the embryo. Around the fourth day of incubation, the membrane pushes its way out, but it remains connected to the embryo by a thin stalk. The allantois has a thick network of blood vessels over its surface. As the membrane grows and expands, these blood vessels come close to the inside of the shell.

An egg shell contains many tiny holes, and it is through these holes that oxygen enters from the outside. The blood vessels in the allantois pick up the oxygen and carry it into the embryo's body. At the same time, they carry the waste gas carbon dioxide away from the embryo's body and bring it to the surface of the shell, where it passes out of the egg.

Besides supplying the embryo with oxygen, the allantois has another important job. It serves as a storage place for the waste products left over after the embryo's body uses food from the yolk. If these waste products were not kept inside the allantois, they could damage the developing embryo.

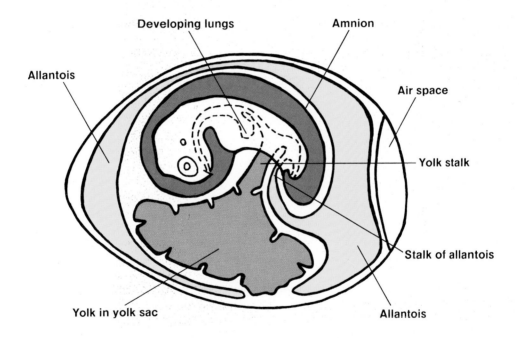

This drawing shows an 11-day embryo inside the egg. The embryo is enclosed by the fluid-filled amnion. Connected to its body is the allantois, which will bring in oxygen from outside the shell until the embryo's lungs are ready to begin working. Also connected to the embryo's body is the yolk sac, which surrounds the yolk.

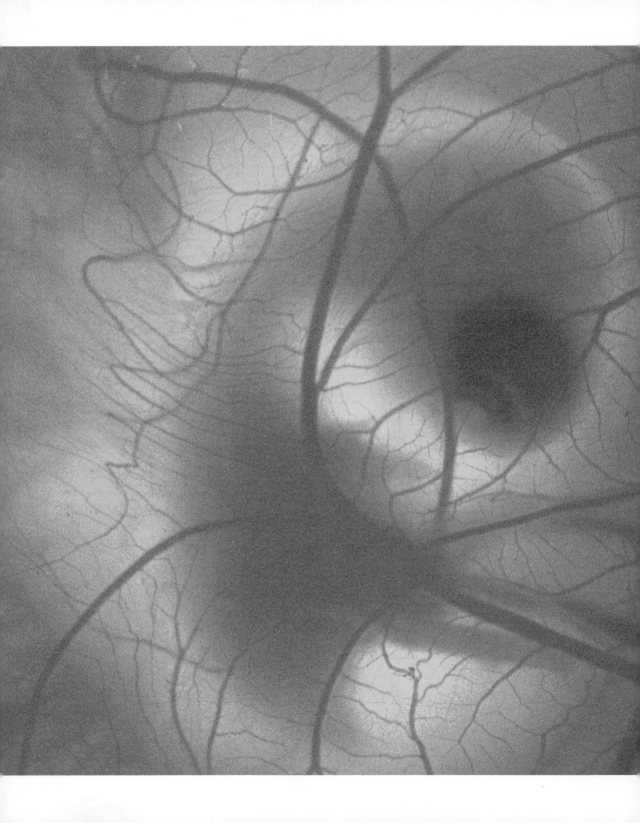

Opposite: A 10-day embryo. *Right*: An 11-day embryo.

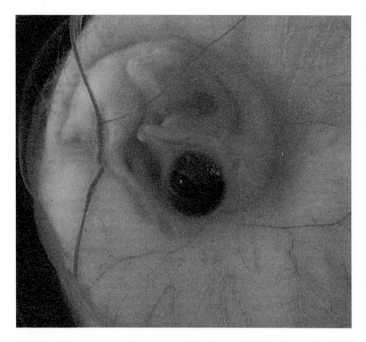

By the time an embryo has been incubated for 10 or 11 days, it has begun to take on a more recognizable shape. In the pictures on these two pages, you can see clearly the head, neck, body, wings, and legs of the developing chick. Particularly noticeable is the large black eye, which is partly covered by an eyelid.

At this stage in its development, the embryo moves around a lot in the shell. The membranes and blood vessels connected to its body twist and turn with it. Another sign of the embryo's rapid growth at this point is the appearance of tiny **feather germs** on its skin. These are the beginnings of the feathers that will eventually cover the chick's body.

35

By the 11th day of incubation, the embryo's eyes have almost completed their development. Some of the different stages in this development are shown in the pictures on the opposite page.

The embryo's eyes begin to grow around the 30th hour of incubation. At this time, they are nothing more than two swellings or pouches on either side of the brain (picture on upper left). These pouches are called the **optic vesicles.**

After about 40 hours, cup-like indentations develop in the outer ends of the optic vesicles (middle left). These are the **optic cups,** and they will eventually become the embryo's eyeballs.

The next part of the eye to appear is the lens, which develops in the opening of the optic cup by the third day of incubation (lower left). As the embryo continues to grow, the other parts of the eye develop from the cells in and around the cup (upper right).

The eyelids are the last parts of the eyes to appear. By the ninth day, they have begun to cover the embryo's large black eyes (middle right). After an embryo has been incubated for 13 days, its eyes are completely closed (lower right).

With its eyes protected by eyelids and tiny feathers beginning to sprout all over its body, a 13-day embryo has only 8 more days of development before it hatches from the egg.

THE DEVELOPMENT OF A CHICK'S EYES

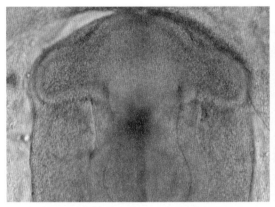

30 hours—the optic vesicles appear.

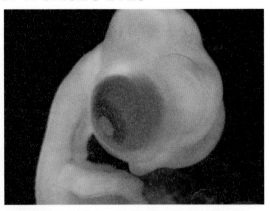

7 days—the eyeball takes shape.

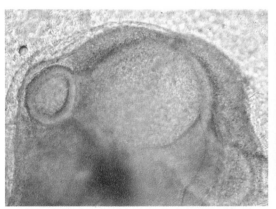

40 hours—the optic cups form.

9 days—the eyelid forms.

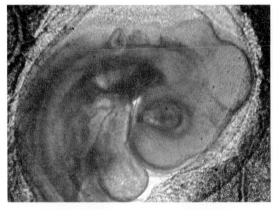

3 days—the lens develops.

13 days—the eye closes.

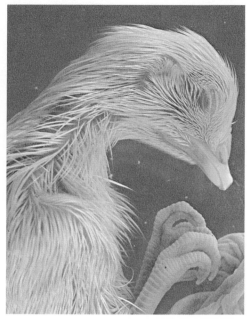

Above: This newly hatched cuckoo has very few feathers. *Right*: A 16-day chicken embryo is covered with tiny feathers.

Sixteen days after incubation began, a chick embryo has fine feathers called **down** all over its body. Even though its feathers are completely grown, the chick will not hatch for another five days. Yet there are many baby birds that leave their eggs before they have any feathers. The young of wild birds like robins, orioles, and woodpeckers are almost featherless when they hatch. They are also blind, and they depend completely on their parents to feed them and keep them warm.

Birds that hatch without feathers go through a long period of development in the nest. It usually takes several weeks before their feathers grow in and they are strong enough to begin flying.

Other wild birds have all their feathers when they hatch. For example, young ducks, pheasants, and grouse leave their eggs fully feathered. These baby birds are strong and are able to move around soon after hatching. Many of them can also find their own food.

Such well-developed baby birds usually belong to species that build their nests on the ground rather than in trees. Ground-nesting birds face many more dangers than birds that live in trees. They must be able to leave the nest soon after hatching to avoid being attacked by predators. Since chickens are related to ground-nesting wild birds, it is not surprising that young chickens are completely developed when they hatch.

Young grouse are able to move around and look for food soon after hatching.

After 18 days of incubation, the growing chick has used up most of the yolk. Just before the chick hatches, any remaining yolk will be drawn inside its body. At the same time, the chick will swallow what is left of the albumen.

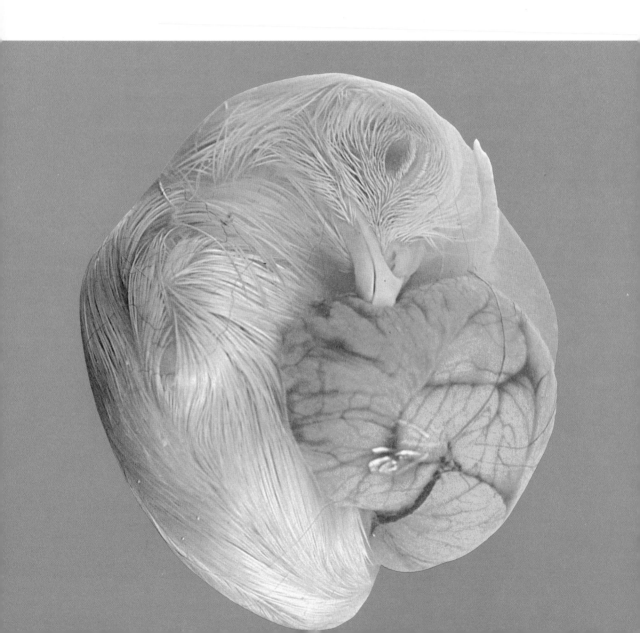

This chick is almost ready to hatch. It will use its sharp egg tooth (indicated by the arrow) to break out of the shell.

Both of these substances will provide nourishment after the chick hatches.

As the time for hatching comes closer, the chick becomes so big that it fills the whole egg. Its development is almost complete, and it has everything it needs to survive in the outside world. The chick even has a special tool to help it get out of the egg. This is the **egg tooth,** a sharp bump near the end of its beak that it will use to break through the shell.

On the 20th day of incubation, one final step is taken. The chick pushes its beak into the air space, a pocket of air at the broad end of the egg that has been sealed off by the inner shell membrane. Up until this time, the chick has been getting oxygen through the blood vessels of the allantois. Now its lungs begin to take over the job of respiration by breathing in the air stored in the air space.

Finally the 21st day arrives, and the first small opening appears in the egg...

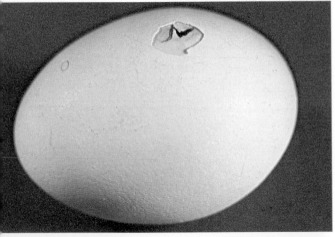

To begin hatching, the chick pokes a hole in the shell with its sharp egg tooth.

Turning around inside the egg, the chick breaks the shell in a line starting at the hole.

Chirping loudly, the chick pushes with its body and feet to widen the opening in the shell.

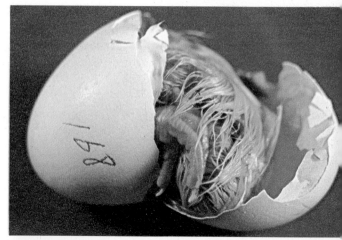

Finally the shell breaks in two pieces, and the chick hatches.

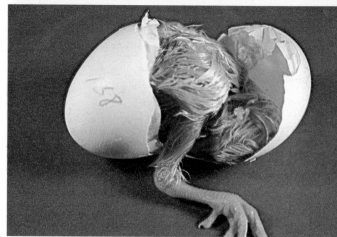

The chick sticks out its legs and pulls the rest of its body out of the shell.

Exhausted after its hard work, the newly hatched chick takes a rest before beginning its new life.

Newly hatched chicks in a hatchery

While the chick rests, its wet feathers begin to dry out. In about two hours, they are completely dry and fluffy. By this time, the chick has become very active, hopping around on its big clawed feet and pecking at everything within reach.

Even after the hard work of hatching, the chick needs no food. It can live for two days on the remains of the yolk and the albumen stored inside its body. When these two days are over, the chick will start to eat and to grow rapidly. In six months, the fluffy little chick will be a sleek full-grown chicken.

GLOSSARY

air space—a pocket of air at the broad end of an egg, located between the inner and outer shell membranes

albumen (al-BYU-mun)—the clear substance surrounding the yolk of an egg. The albumen protects the embryo and also serves as a source of food.

allantois (eh-LAN-twus)—the membrane that supplies oxygen to the embryo and stores waste material

amnion (AM-nee-ahn)—the membrane that forms a transparent sack surrounding the embryo

amniotic fluid (am-nee-AHT-ik)—the liquid that fills the amnion and in which the embryo floats

chalaza (kuh-LAY-zuh)—a twisted piece of albumen that connects the yolk to the inner shell membrane

cloaca (klo-AY-kuh)—an opening in a chicken's body that is connected to the reproductive system

down—the fine, soft feathers of baby birds

egg tooth—a sharp bump near the end of a chick's beak, used to break through the shell. The egg tooth falls off after the chick hatches.

embryo (EM-bree-oh)—an animal in an early stage of development, before birth or hatching

feather germ—the early stage in the development of a chick's feathers

fertilization—the union of a male and a female sex cell

hen—a female chicken

incubation—keeping an egg at the proper temperature so that it will hatch

incubator—a machine that keeps large numbers of eggs at the proper temperature so that they will hatch. The temperature in an electric incubator is usually between 99 and 101 degrees Fahrenheit (36°-38°C).

46

membrane—a thin, flexible sheet of cells. Several different membranes play a part in the development of a chicken embryo.

notochord (NOTE-uh-kord)—a line of cells that marks the area where an embryo's spinal cord develops

nucleus—the most important part of a cell, containing the material that controls growth and cell division

optic cup—a cup-like indentation in the optic vesicle that develops into the embryo's eyeball

optic vesicle (VES-ih-kul)—a pouch or swelling on either side of the head that is the first stage in the development of an embryo's eyes.

ovary—an organ that produces female sex cells

oviduct (OH-vih-dukt)—a tube through which eggs pass on their way out of a hen's body

ovum—a female sex cell

rooster—a male chicken

somites (SO-mites)—block-like clusters of cells that appear on either side of the notochord early in an embryo's development. The cells of the somites eventually become the muscles and bones of the embryo's body

sperm—a male sex cell

testes (TES-teez)—organs that produce male sex cells

yolk—the part of an egg that supplies food for the developing embryo

yolk sac (SAK)—a membrane that surrounds the yolk and connects it to the embryo's body

yolk stalk—a thin section of the yolk sac that is connected to the embryo's body

INDEX